A letter to you!

This book has been a labor of love unlike anything else. Sara and I have put our hearts and souls into creating a whole new world for us to explore with all of you. Tears of joy, and tears of frustration dollop each page. We would love to express our deepest gratitude for you spending time with your loved ones and using our book as a way to spend quality time together. We hope this series will help guide your way with conversations, and help strengthen your bonds together. We look forward to sharing the journey and more wonders with all of you. We truly cannot express how thankful we are for this amazing opportunity we only could dream of before.

Never stop wondering.
-Zia and Sara

From the author,

This book is dedicated to my amazingly supportive wife Jaime, and my best friend Sami. Both have never stopped believing in me and always encouraged me to keep creating.

I would like to dedicate this book to my wonderful husband, Brandon, and our four beautiful children. I would like to also dedicate this book to my parents, Michael and Tammy Smith. You inspired my love for creating and art.

From the illustrator,

Paperback: ISBN 978-1-304-94209-8

First paperback edition October 2021

lulu

Jaime Wonders

About the Tooth Fairy!

This is Jaime! Jaime is always curious, and always asking questions. Jaime likes to learn how things work or why we do certain things.

Jaime has learned many things, like why we use a fork.

Because otherwise eating spaghetti would be really messy!

Jaime also learned why we put away our toys when we're done playing with them.

Because they can go missing or we can trip and get hurt.

But then Jaime asked the grown ups a question that they did not know the answer to.

"Why does the Tooth Fairy take my baby teeth?"

"I'm not sure. Maybe we should write the Tooth Fairy a letter and ask her."

So that's exactly what Jaime did!

The letter was placed under her pillow the next time Jaime

lost a tooth.

The next morning, Jaime sprang awake and threw the pillow to the floor and saw a letter back from the Tooth Fairy!

Dear Jaime,
I will stop by
and tell your
family all about
what I do with
your baby teeth.
I will see you after
you eat breakfast.
T*Fairy

Breakfast couldn't come fast enough! Jaime ate breakfast and as soon as all the food was gone...

The Tooth Fairy was at the door right on time!

Poof!

"Good morning, everyone! Let me tell you why I take your baby teeth."

"I don't collect only baby teeth. I actually collect all of your favorite things when you outgrow them."

"Things like your favorite blanket, teddy bears and stuffed animals, and even toys and special things that you made yourself!"

"Teeth are very special. It shows that your body is growing up big and strong! I know it can be scary sometimes to lose your teeth, which is why I leave a present for you being so brave."

"After I collect something, I take it to Heaven. I put all of your things into a very special museum all about you and your life!"

"When you go to Heaven, all of your friends and family that are there greet you and walk you through your personal museum and see all of your memories you created in your life."

"So next time you have to say goodbye to something you love because you are outgrowing it, remember I will put it in your museum. You will get to see and play with everything again in Heaven. You can't get new things without getting rid of your old things.
That's why we celebrate growing up!"

TINA

KITTY

"Wow!" Jaime exclaimed. "So the baby tooth you took last night will be in my very own museum!"

"That's so cool! I can't wait to grow up and add more things to my museum!"

"I look forward to seeing you grow up, Jaime!"

The next time Jaime outgrew a toy, no crying happened. Jaime knew that toy would be waiting in Heaven, and a new toy would help Jaime grow up.

Now that you know all about the Tooth Fairy, and your museum in Heaven, what are you looking forward to putting in your museum? Write it down here, and put this book under your pillow so the Tooth Fairy will know items you are ready for her to take!

_____

_____

_____

Jaime Wonders is actually based on an incident when Zia was a child! He asked his mother what the Tooth Fairy does with the baby teeth she collects. His mother decided to ask him what *he* thinks the Tooth Fairy does with the teeth. The base for the story is what Zia came up with the very next day.

That idea stayed with Zia until he decided to write a children's book about it! With no idea what to do with the story, it just sat, untouched for 5+ years; until a podcast called Buddycast interviewed Aaron Ozee, author of the children's book "*Regulus*". Zia reached out to Aaron to ask for advice about getting his Tooth Fairy story out to the world. Without Buddycast and Aaron's generosity, Zia's story may never have left his tablet.

About the Author:

Hey kids! My name is Zia, and I wrote this story, Jaime Wonders About the Tooth Fairy! I'm an award winning balloon artist and performer. My mother's work inspired me to follow my dreams of performing, but I've also always had a love for writing. I've put that love into writing routines for my magic shows, and now I've put it in this story to share with you!

About the Illustrator:

Hi! My name is Sara. I drew the pictures! I hope you and your families will enjoy watching Jaime's first adventure in our series! I had so much fun bringing it to life. I have four children of my own: a son and three daughters! Elias, Kaylie, Madeline, and Jayden. I wonder what they will find in their museums(and mine)!

Special credits from the illustrator!

These character designs were inspired by people I hold very dear.

The parents in this book are based on my own!

This is Tammy and Mike!

The Grown Ups

And the Tooth Fairy was based on a very close friend's mother; Annie!

The Toothfairy

And the star of the show!

Jaime!

Jaime is actually based on Zia's wife!

Special thanks to...

Zia Quill Kay would like to thank the following people:

My parents, Kelly and Zack Martinez
My grandparents Lois and Ed Krochmalny
My aunt Whitney Krochmalny
My amazing friends, Dennis and Lisa Fogleman
Aaron Ozee, author of the kids book Regulus
Nick Sorensen, creator of Buddycast
Scotty Cranmer, pro bmx legend
Francis and Linda Murillo owners of Murillo's Mexican Restaurant
Tim Yearnshaw, my fifth grade teacher
Lajuana Bryan my high school English teacher
Dave Elliot mass media teacher
Erik Dresden friend who is more like family.
Fredrick Lee amazing friend
Valerie Renesto another amazing friend!
Isaiah Robinson & Barrett Harrington friends since elementary school
Matt Andrade close friend since high school
Josh Martin so close, it's like we're conjoined twins
Brandon Morgan best roommate ever
Micah and Heidi Stuber friends, and amazing teachers
Amy Jarvis friend is is more like family
Stag Nechtan buddy since middle school
Wayne Houchin amazing friend, and just as amazing as a magician
Chris Cook director at Green Valley Theater Company
Cody Stark host of Goodday Sacramento
Paul Vigil inspiration magician
Anthony Malchar top notch balloon artist, and friend
Fred Harshberger friend and balloon art instructor
Vivian De Jesus balloon artist and friend.

Sara Clemons would like to give a special thank you to her dear friend
Desmond Nadeau for his crucial help in assembling the book.

We couldn't have done this without you Dj.
Thank you!

Made in the USA
Las Vegas, NV
17 March 2023